On Fire

Robert Mercer-Nairne

GRITPOUL

Illustrations by Marisa Attard (marisa@onvol.net)

Layout by Scancraft Studios (M) Ltd., G. Abos Street, l-Iklin BZN 11, MALTA.

Photography by Mangion Studio, 9a Naxxar Road, San Gwann, SGN08, MALTA.

Printed by Friesens Corp., One Printer's Way, Altona, Manitoba R0G 0B0, CANADA.

Produced by Gritpoul, Meikleour House, Meikleour, Perthshire, PH2 6EA, SCOTLAND.

Published by Gritpoul, Inc., 10900NE 8th, 900, Bellevue, WA 98004-4448, USA.

For all of us -

who must remember

Contents

Foreword

This is the second of what will be three small books of poems or, as I prefer to call them, word pictures. The first, *Mercer-Nairne In Malta*, drew its inspiration from my island home. This second, *On Fire*, also draws on Maltese life but during the year in which I wrote the poems, three themes emerged. The most general is our relationship to fire. It consumes us, sustains us and makes possible our re-birth (through the cycle of life). The second theme arises out of the injuries we inflict upon ourselves and one another, largely as a result of incomplete perspectives. The third is the fine line we must tread between order and chaos, good and evil, hope and despair - opposites central to the human condition which, I think, can only be mediated by compassion.

Blind cord flapping in the wind points to the pervasiveness of the primal energy that started our universe and continues to influence every aspect of our lives. *When the time comes* is both a letting go and an acknowledgment that we have an inescapable place within existence. That seems to me a comforting thought. In *The final act* we see the link between destruction and creation. Some seeds, for example, only germinate when touched by fire. Fire can destroy old life and create the conditions for new life, a seemingly perverse transformation central to all experience.

September 11th, A time to mourn and *The trail* touch on conflict and our reaction to it. We often overlook the fact that a violent act is only one side of an event. The other side is how we respond. Violence can beget violence and frequently does. But if we choose, we can react in many different ways.

In *Wasteland* and *Singer* life asserts itself in the face of emptiness. In the first we are asked to recognize that progress should only be a means to an end, not an end in itself. In the second, a desperate man in a war torn landscape hears a girl's voice and is revived.

But as *Fish pond* suggests, blind happiness can be just as dangerous. Mankind's lot is not a simple one.

The General, the Law and Compassion has two old friends arguing. It would be nice to think that every issue could be resolved over a glass of wine, but until we learn to put our shared humanity above our perceived self-interest, I don't see it happening. All too frequently we appear to need the experience of confrontation (which may lead to us winning or losing) in order to see what, in time, becomes self-evident. Imagine a narrow mountain track. On one side sheer rock. On the other a chasm. The guardians of order say concentrate on the rock face. The revolutionary says jump and be free!

The point of *Purpose* is to try and find the humanity in us - the spirit, or essence. The rock face and the chasm do not really offer much and a narrow mountain track can be pretty depressing, mile after mile. Unless we think we will reach a verdant valley - a promised land - the journey is hard to sustain. But supposing the promised land is inside us?

The other word pictures speak for themselves. I put *A Child's day* last because it is about fun and hope. Life will present us with enough trials, without the ideologue in us trying to impose them. Give me innocent wonder over fierce certainty, every time.

Once again, Marisa Attard has done the words proud. Her drawings delight.

Robert Mercer-Nairne
Malta - 2004.

Blind cord,
flapping in the wind.

I watched the blind cord

Flapping in the wind,

Clack, clack - clack,

Twisting wildly,

Full of life.

To think it is a ripple

From the primal cauldron

That blew its energy into all things

And gave **us** life,

Is strange.

Out of the cave.

Out of the cave
I could see
A wide expanse of sea.
In the middle
A single yacht,
In high summer stillness,
Moved across the water.

Just once,
I caught the sound
Of a man and woman,
Drifting through the air.
Full sail;
Imperceptible motion.

Lap, lap for them.
Silence for me.
Bliss for us both.

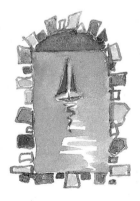

Gone fishing.

Gone fishing,
Pole and bait in hand.
Gone wishing,
It's better to sit than stand.
A day of dreams,
A day of nothing,
A day of cast and pull.
A day of nibbled bait
And blissful wait,
Of basking in the sun.
Come fishy.
Fishy, come!
I have fed you maggot stew.
To show my wife what I have done -
Please!
A little one will do.

When the time comes.

When the time comes

I will lie there

Somewhere

In the sun.

And as its rays shroud me in gentle heat,

And my body slows and cools,

I will let my spirit float away

Up the sunbeam of existence,

Back into the womb of life.

Crumpled walnut.

Walking down the street,
I nearly missed her,
Staring out
From her doorway,
Like a crumpled walnut,
Behind a plastic sheet.

Her fuzzy window
Let her see the world,
Protected from the rain,
Through those sharp eyes
That held me tight
For just a second,
As I passed by.

You cried once, old woman;
You loved once, old woman;
You felt all those things
I too have felt.

And in your eyes,
Your fierce brown eyes,
I felt,
For just that second,
You.

Watch me!

Watch me!
Olympic diver me.
Crouched on the rock
Next to the sea.

Watch me!
Hands pointed,
Head down,
Coiled like a spring.

Watch me!
I am diving,
Me.
Splash.

Thrash, gurgle, gasp.
Did you see me?
Did you see!
I nearly dove.

Yes darling,
Yes!
Head first,
Next time.

The bee and the rose bud.

*D*ancing girl, dance -
Flashing sequins.
Sparkle girl, sparkle -
Silky fresh.
Rose bud girl,
Tight bundled expectation,
Driving the bees crazy -
Wanting.
One day
You will open
And a bee will drink his fill.
Until then
Swinging girl, swing
And drive those hornets mad.

*S*tung girl, stung -
Sweet confusion.
Cling girl, cling -
Burning touch.
Flaming girl,
Open to infinity,
Driving yourself crazy -
Wanting.
One bee
Buzzing madly
Dominates your every hour,
In passionate expectation.
Quiver girl, quiver
And drink the draught of life.

Andy's retirement.

*O*ot a bed Andy.
It's yer last day.
Aye, it is, Margaret.
I'll soon be away.
I hay yer sandwich
O' the table.
That's bra.
What's inside?
Bacon an' cheese,
Wi' a pickle.
Guid enough lass.
Guid enough.

*T*hese two have led good lives;
Ploughed a straight furrow.
As parents,
In their church,
They have set their standards high.
Now it is time for Autumn
And just desserts,
Richly earned.
It is the quality of men that matters.
Not power
And not worth.

The final act.

*T*hese two know the end is near.
The gusting winds of circumstance
Have come at last
To claim their just reward.
As transforming heat
Breaks open their carapace,
A violent contortion
Bends them out
And in,
Every sinew gripped
Each opening explored.
With one last rush of desperation,
They cling
And thrust
And join.
A final act
Of life-confirming consummation.

*S*pent, dishevelled, exhausted,
They lie.
Their seed spilt out
In glistening abandon.
From old to new,
In gasping roughness,
Existence is reborn.

Butterfly.

*E*ndoscopic

Entropy

Fan hour to hour.

Bright colored

Fibrillate

From flower to flower.

The sweet spot.

*W*e often find peace
Before and after,
In that space between,
Where a calm beauty
Takes over our souls.
When we live
At one,
And go about life's tasks
In gentle busyness.

Today,
Even the bay
Is still.

A fisher fishes,
A boat comes and goes,
A dog barks,
And a woman admonishes,
Unconvincingly,
From a bar.

Summer is over,
Winter not yet begun.
We wait in the sweet spot,
Free from labors past,
And labors still to come.
Suspended time,
In paradise.

Fish pond.

Green, orange,
Mostly green.
Darting orange,
Green weed, green grass,
Flashes of orange.
As the fish swim around their domain
It is the fish you notice
But the domain that matters.

Like the goldfish
In their green kingdom,
Do we notice ourselves too much
And our domain too little?
If we will not submit to God
We should at least act like him;
Feeling the whole
And not just the part.

Flames beneath the surface
Swirl in choreographed excitement,
As lips probe the upper limits
Grasping nature's bounty.
Splash!
Happy fish, feed away.
Your pond has sprung a leak
And will be dry one day.

September 11th.

Fall.
Blue sky.
New York morning.
Bang.
One of the Twin Towers is hit.
Hit!
Smoke. Flames.
Emergency services scramble.
Cameras gather.
Christ.
That plane's going to hit....
It has hit the other Tower.
Oh, hell.
People are jumping.
Thud.
Keep out of the way!
Keep out of the way!

Let the emergency services through.
Stand to the right.
Let us pass.
Get down to the street.
Smoke.
Burned people.
It's collapsing!
The South Tower is collapsing.
Millions across the world
Stare in horror
As half the World Trade Center
Crumbles to the ground.

We're getting reports.
Reports of people calling on their cell phones
From the planes.
They're stabbing the crew with knives.
What shall I do?
Oh God.
The second Tower is collapsing.
We had 300 of our people in there
The best from Rescue 1,
The Mayor says, who was at the scene.

Report just in.
The Pentagon's been hit!
An American Airlines 757
Flew in below me
A man
From an apartment opposite
Explains.

The President is leaving Florida.
He was visiting a school.
Is he coming to Washington?
Yes.
No.
A fourth plane has come down.
Near Pittsburgh.
Was it aiming for Camp David?

Again and again,
The image of United Flight 175
Hitting the South Tower
Saturates our minds.

The President is coming through live
From a bunker
In Strategic Air Command,
Nebraska.
Freedom will be defended.
He tells us.
As people recount their stories
To a gasping world.

I was in the building.
I was in the street.
I have friends there.
I am a Christian
And I know I'm supposed to love.
But it's real hard.
I hope they get the pigs.
Politicians and statesmen,
Old and new,
Are interviewed.
I am glad we will not distinguish
Between terrorists and the countries that
                                    harbor them.

They say.
This is war!

New Yorkers line up
To give blood
At every hospital.
Tens of thousands worked in those buildings
We are told.
But no one wants to estimate the dead.

It is a crime
Too horrific to contemplate.
A homicide or rape
You grasp.
But mass murder?
Numbers are just numbers.
It is the individuals behind them that count.
For the whole,
It is our way of life
Our freedom
Which has been attacked.
Let us hope
That vengeance
Does not lead us to compound
The infamy of this day.

A time to mourn.

*F*irst,
Let us mourn
Those so suddenly gone,
Many without trace.
No more touch,
No more sound,
No more smell.
At least they cannot feel our pain.

*T*hose who kill
Wound the living,
Not the dead.
So it is up to us,
The wounded ones,
To build anew
And stop this evil in its tracks.
Not out of bitterness,
But out of pride
In the ones we loved and lost.

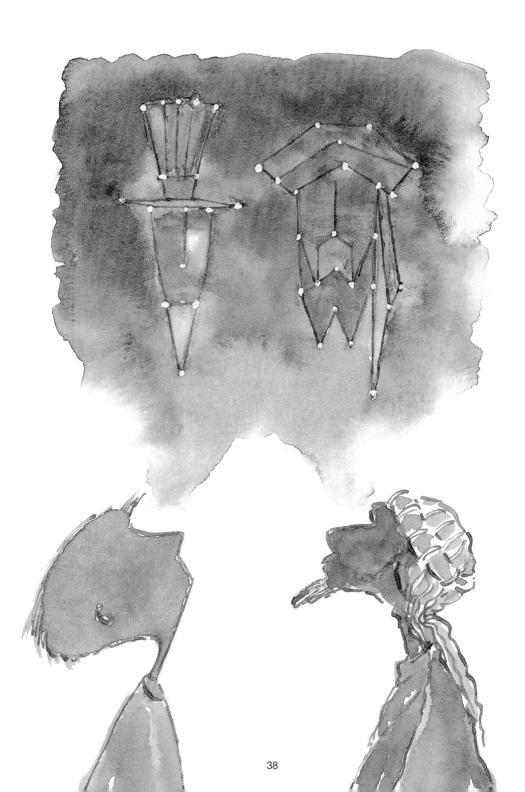

The trail.

These men are suspects.
They were there.
They had the means
And their origin
Suggests the motive.
At the head,
A sinister man
And in between,
Hatred.

All we have to do is find the trail.
Dot to dot,
And the picture of our fears will form.
But the trail!
If we followed the trail,
We would find
That part of it
Led back to us.

Wasteland.

We have split the atom,
Sent probes to Mars,
But what have we achieved,
In the greater order of things?

Every need we ascertain,
From conquest to reproduction,
Has acted as a spur
To technological innovation
And change.

But are things better?
And if so, how?
What qualities have we mastered?
What qualities have we ignored?

These questions are important.
Because unless we understand
What we are part of,
And take the whole forward
And not just our shallow selves,
We will end up in a technological wasteland
That possesses everything
Save the one thing we yearn for most,
And that is Life.

Singer.

Sing, sing,
Singer girl,
Sing.
Up,
Drawn out
And down.
Your sweet honeysuckle melody;
Caress, calm, arouse.
Rhythm bop,
Silky sound,
Absorb, amour, carouse.
Long-legged dream time;
Majestic mystery of love.
Female note
Exploded,
Into a thousand particles of human life,
Dancing in my heart.

The General, the Law and Compassion.

They are going to try the General for
                                    murder!

The General?
For murder?
All generals are trained to murder!
We do not call it that, certainly
We call it 'defending our country's
honor'.

But the junta deposed the elected
                                    leadership.

The <u>elected</u>
Leadership.
That must have been a criminal act?
Our soldiers swear to defend
Our country and all its institutions.

Suppose an elected leader tries to
                                    undermine
Institutions
We hold dear.
If our liberal democracy
Is being changed to a Marxist State,
What exactly should all our brave soldiers
                                    do?

We cannot be sure if that was Allende's
                                        plan.

There was chaos,
Disruption,
And our economy was in shreds.
The electors would have thrown him out.
The generals did not need to take control.

Remember Germany's Hitler? He was
                                        elected.

Mighty Führer!
Chancellor!
But, like Stalin, he became the head
Of a totalitarian state.
How many souls then and since have wished
That the soldier von Stauffenberg had
                                        prevailed?

But those two evil men were monsters pure
                                        and simple.

Allende.
Pinochet.
These two were in a different league.
One, I grant you, was incompetent.
But the other usurped power that was not
                                        his.

No, Communism rode on the incompetent's back,
Unscrupulous,
Ambitious,
And the army acted just in time.
The civil war was bloody and cruel
And we must mourn all those who
                                needlessly died.

But torture? Why torture? Where are all
                                the disappeared?
The broken hearts,
Broken lives.
Sons and daughters taken without trial,
And interrogated with pain
Until their flesh was fit only for the worms.

Every civil war is the most uncivil of things.
Yours is over.
Let it be.
Praise the young who fought for their
                                beliefs.
But honor this general you charge.
Your country is free and strong. He served
                                you well.

Yes. He was a fine general. I will grant you
that.

Above the law?
No. Not that!
But the law is the law of the State.
Undermine the State and lose the law.
The law is only what we choose to defend.

That is my point. For this the general must
be tried.

To show that we
Hold law dear.
Your law was killed when politics failed,
When those elected broke people's trust.
To apply it now is to re-start the fight.

Heaven prevent us from doing that, my dear
old friend!

Oh, I agree!
Then, a drink!
To your good law and my general!
And to this rich friendship that binds us.
Yes. Without compassion we will always
fail.

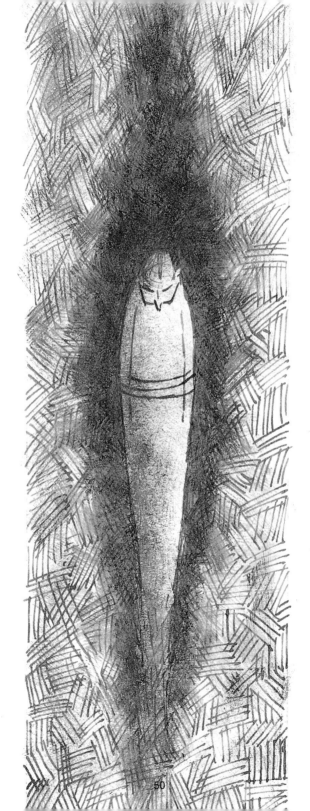

Purpose.

We forever wonder
Why?
The feeling of utter disconnect
Which makes death appear
A pleasant state,
An end to desperate anguish
Draining dry men's souls.
The ebb and flow of stimulus,
In and out,
Of confirmation
And non-confirmation,
Of use
And uselessness.
Only the brave or lost
Live other than in different men's eyes.

The crushing abandonment of the State:
The systematic hatred
Which defines one
And casts out another,
Into a land of utter purgatory,
Empty even of flames for company.
Would that you could claim to be a sinner,
Something - anything.
Instead you inhabit nothing,
A blank blackness of despair,
Devoid of purpose.

*S*o what is purpose,
If it can be destroyed so cheaply?
A puffed up edifice
Of self congratulation,
Of tasks set and achieved,
Of rules made and followed,
Of goals and their fulfilment,
Of endless self-satisfied back scratchings?
Or is it survival?
If so, none of us do that for long.

Does the animal need purpose to run?
The plant purpose to flower?
Or the butterfly a purpose to its zigzag
                                        way?
Consciousness and freedom are terrible
                                        things.
They make one think.
They make one choose.
Did God throw us out of Eden for a
                                        purpose?

Or was it anger?

Surely, our purpose is to expand what is
                                    good,

To fight what is evil
And to make our world a lovelier place?
Not an Eden of ignorant bliss,
But a world of ceaseless discovery
In which compassion, joy and fun abound.
Perhaps we love ourselves too much
And love too little.

But wait!
Have I not missed something?
What about the cut and thrust of
                                    competition,
The spur that drives us on,
To make those changes
Without which we would not progress?
Are death, fear and destruction
Lesser tools on our journey of self-discovery,
Than life, love and compassion?
Or, do we need them both?
Opposite sides of a tension
That is the spring of life.
Are not moments of peace just that,
Moments,
Along the jagged path of life
Driven by a desire
Both to conquer and preserve?

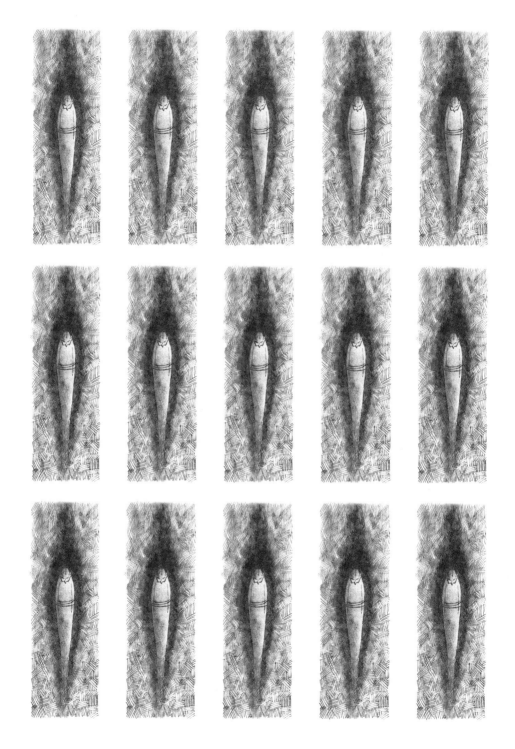

Our purpose *is* survival
But not a petty survival
Like that of the worm;
Not an industrious survival
Like that of the ant;
Not a conquering survival
Like that of the lion;
Not even a beautiful survival -
There are far more beautiful things
Than we will ever be -
But a survival that requires us to look death
Squarely in the eye.

So do not ignore the desperate man
The man who has lost all hope
The one for whom there is nothing
But a blackness deep and dark.
In his soul there was a light once
Just like the light in yours
Which you will find,
If you search hard.

Should you see him suffer,
And yet do nothing to ease his pain,
You are far closer to his misery than you
                                        think.

As was his, your purpose is to lead a noble
                                          life
A life enhancing life.
Do not squander
Your one and only chance.
You exist to express the full potential of our
                                          universe
In a different way
And on a different plane.
Not a petty mean-minded thing is this,
But a great thing,
A wonderful thing,
An unfolding thing,
A thing of richness, beauty, courage,
                        compassion and belief.
What greater purpose could there be?

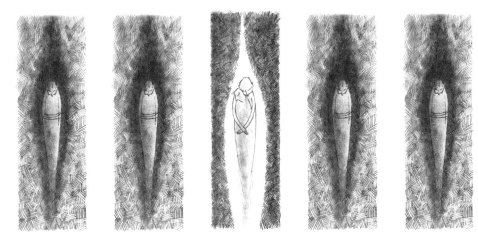

A Child's day.

Ding dong merrily on.....
High.
High as a kite.
Champagne flowing,
Log fire glowing.
Good King Wenceslas
Ho, ho-ing.
I love turkey,
The bird.
Good wife,
Good bird.
Come children,
Come.
Watch your parents play.
This is your day,
A Child's day.
We are that child,
Today.

Also by Robert Mercer-Nairne
    Poetry
        Mercer-Nairne In Malta (2002)
        Getting Married (2005)
    Fiction
        The Letter Writer (2004)
        Like No Other (2005)